Well-Connected

by Mary Ellen Hopkins

#4 $\frac{3}{4}$

ME Publications

1995

Dedication

To Jennifer Ellen Hopkins
with love,
Grandma Hopkins

Other Books Available from ME Publications

It's Okay If You Sit On My Quilt
Double Wedding Ring
Bakers Dozen Doubled
Hidden Wells
A Log Cabin Notebook
Connecting Up
Continuing On
Over Under Double-Disconnected

ME Publications

Special thanks to Kaye England and Anne Gallo; without whose help this book would not have been possible.
Graphic design & layout by Kevin Britton of Great Britton Graphics, Indianapolis, Indiana
Photography by Michael Negley, Los Angeles, California

Direct inquiries to ME Publications, PO Box 1288, Cardiff, CA 92007
(800) 527-2665, Printed in Korea

Table of Contents

Conversation With Mary Ellen

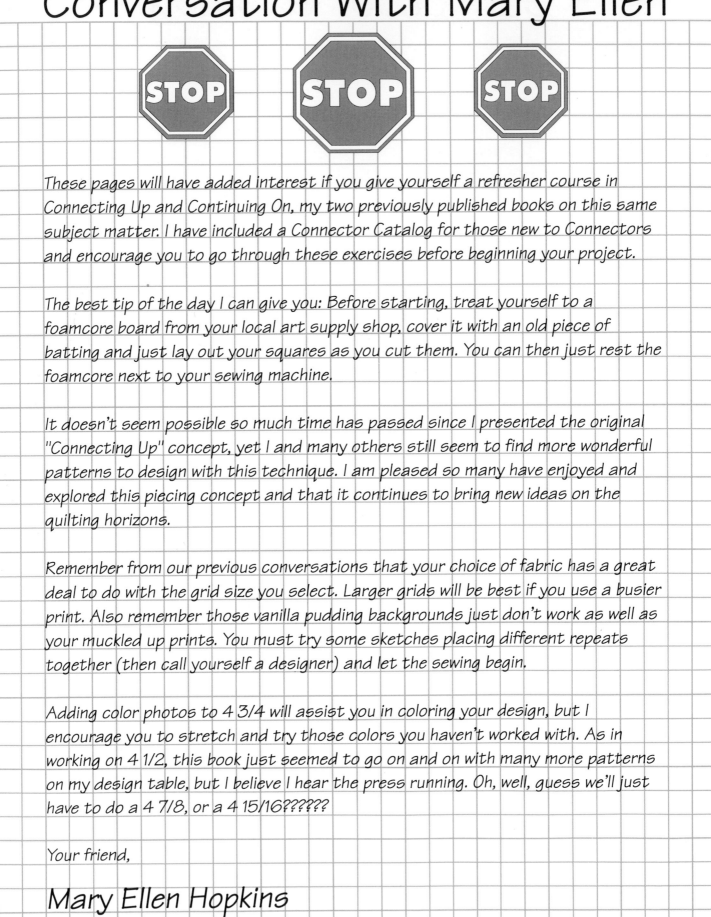

These pages will have added interest if you give yourself a refresher course in Connecting Up and Continuing On, my two previously published books on this same subject matter. I have included a Connector Catalog for those new to Connectors and encourage you to go through these exercises before beginning your project.

The best tip of the day I can give you: Before starting, treat yourself to a foamcore board from your local art supply shop, cover it with an old piece of batting and just lay out your squares as you cut them. You can then just rest the foamcore next to your sewing machine.

It doesn't seem possible so much time has passed since I presented the original "Connecting Up" concept, yet I and many others still seem to find more wonderful patterns to design with this technique. I am pleased so many have enjoyed and explored this piecing concept and that it continues to bring new ideas on the quilting horizons.

Remember from our previous conversations that your choice of fabric has a great deal to do with the grid size you select. Larger grids will be best if you use a busier print. Also remember those vanilla pudding backgrounds just don't work as well as your muckled up prints. You must try some sketches placing different repeats together (then call yourself a designer) and let the sewing begin.

Adding color photos to 4 3/4 will assist you in coloring your design, but I encourage you to stretch and try those colors you haven't worked with. As in working on 4 1/2, this book just seemed to go on and on with many more patterns on my design table, but I believe I hear the press running. Oh, well, guess we'll just have to do a 4 7/8, or a 4 15/16??????

Your friend,

Mary Ellen Hopkins

4

Connector Catalog

If you are using a design block with your Connector block, sew the design block, turn one over and measure raw edge to raw edge of the square you want you Connector corner to line up with:

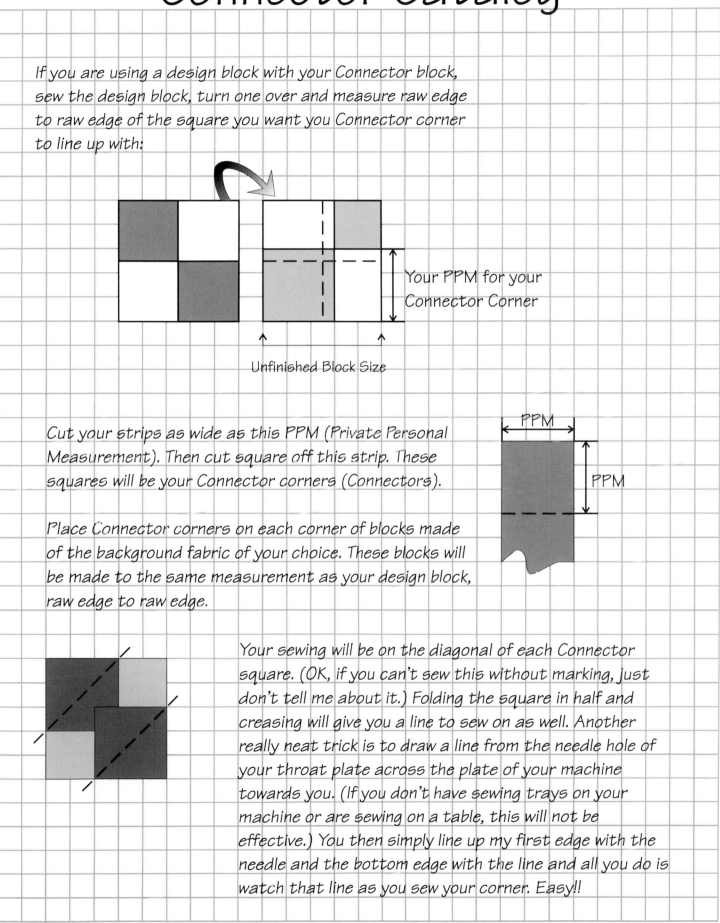

Your PPM for your Connector Corner

Unfinished Block Size

Cut your strips as wide as this PPM (Private Personal Measurement). Then cut square off this strip. These squares will be your Connector corners (Connectors).

Place Connector corners on each corner of blocks made of the background fabric of your choice. These blocks will be made to the same measurement as your design block, raw edge to raw edge.

PPM

PPM

Your sewing will be on the diagonal of each Connector square. (OK, if you can't sew this without marking, just don't tell me about it.) Folding the square in half and creasing will give you a line to sew on as well. Another really neat trick is to draw a line from the needle hole of your throat plate across the plate of your machine towards you. (If you don't have sewing trays on your machine or are sewing on a table, this will not be effective.) You then simply line up my first edge with the needle and the bottom edge with the line and all you do is watch that line as you sew your corner. Easy!!

Connector Catalog, Continued

Now, for the most important part of this process. DO NOT cut your original background corner off! I'm very firm on this matter, and I know many other directions tell you to remove this because of bulk, now let's get real, how many of you are going to hand quilt these Connectors? My point exactly, and the benefits of having that corner to square to is worth dealing with extra bulk. So, only cut the middle layer off.

Another point for leaving that corner...let's assume you didn't sew perfectly straight (I don't believe this) and swept to the inside such as:

You can then bring a corner of the Connector to the corner of your background, press and presto, you have kept your block square. Try this without that background corner and see what you have. Notwithstanding any of these benefits, I simply will not permit you to cut this off (I really am watching over your shoulder when you do this).

Now your Connector and your four-patch will line up when placed side-by-side.

Now there are times I want my Connector to be larger than the square it will adjoin, so I over-Connect, or make the square larger. Not only does this make matching easier but you get a different look. Try this on any of the designs.

Most importantly, remember that to calculate your Connector size you must first determine your PPM of the block you will be joining, or if you are only working with Connectors, simply take half of the cut size plus 1/4" and that is your Connector, i.e. if I cut my square for Kansas City Dugout blocks to 3", half of that is 1 1/2" + 1/4" equals 1 3/4" for my Connector. If I wanted to over-Connect, I would cut the Connector 2". You must play with this concept to find the results most pleasing to you. Remember, this is a **concept**!!!

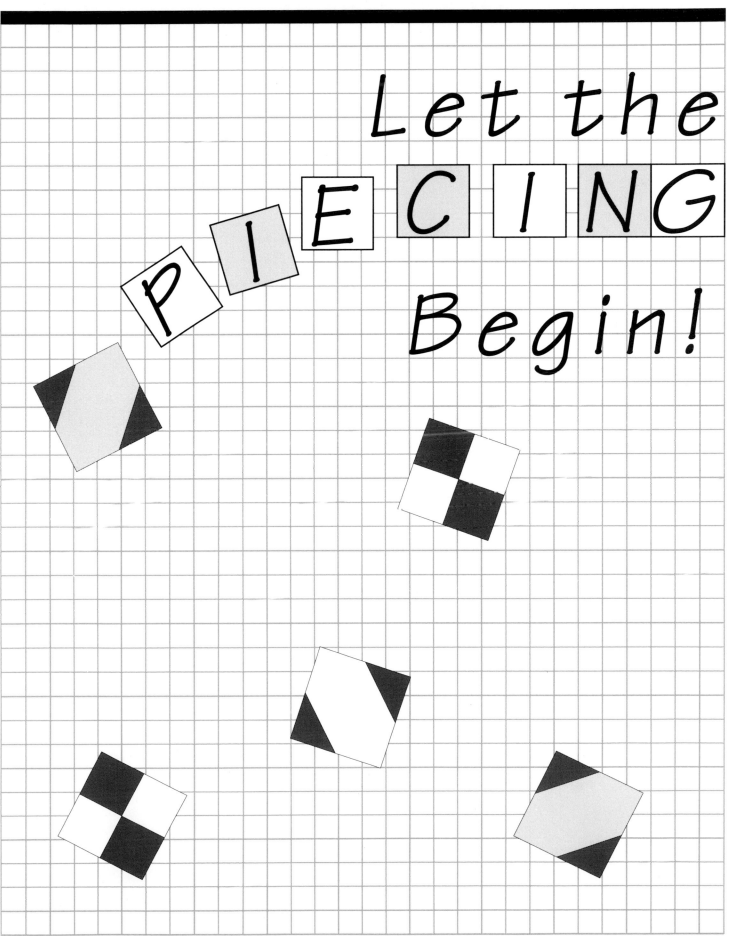

Let the **PIECING** Begin!

Designing with Creative Connectors

Now on to designing with those Creative Connectors.

Kansas City Dugout is very simple piecing, made more complex looking by using the Connector corner.

Your design blocks are only a four-patch...

and a Dugout block...

To calculate this, you would first determine the cut size for the strip width on the four-patch. Assume you cut 1-1/2". Then you would complete your four-patch, measure raw edge to raw edge and that would be the cut size of your background Dugout block, simple so far...then your Connectors would be cut the same as your strip width, in this case 1-1/2". It can't get any easier. Now you want to over-connect? Cut your background for the Dugout block the same just change your Connector square to 1-3/4". Now, to complete the project on the next page you won't need anyone to give you cut sizes, you'll just decide on one and away you go!

WARNING: You may stop cooking and cleaning when you see how much fun you will have connecting!! I cannot be held responsible!!!

Kansas City Dugout

The simplest of piecing! Four-patch and Connectors. Great in the barn-raising set. For extra effect, muckle those backgrounds!

Check out the photos of this quilt. For a more unusual look, each round could be very different or even more planned...you're the designer!

Because the design is so very "simple", the background fabric should change on each round.

Note:
Bullseye is not in the center!

Back Home Again in Kansas City

#3 from page 23, #4 1/2, Continuing On

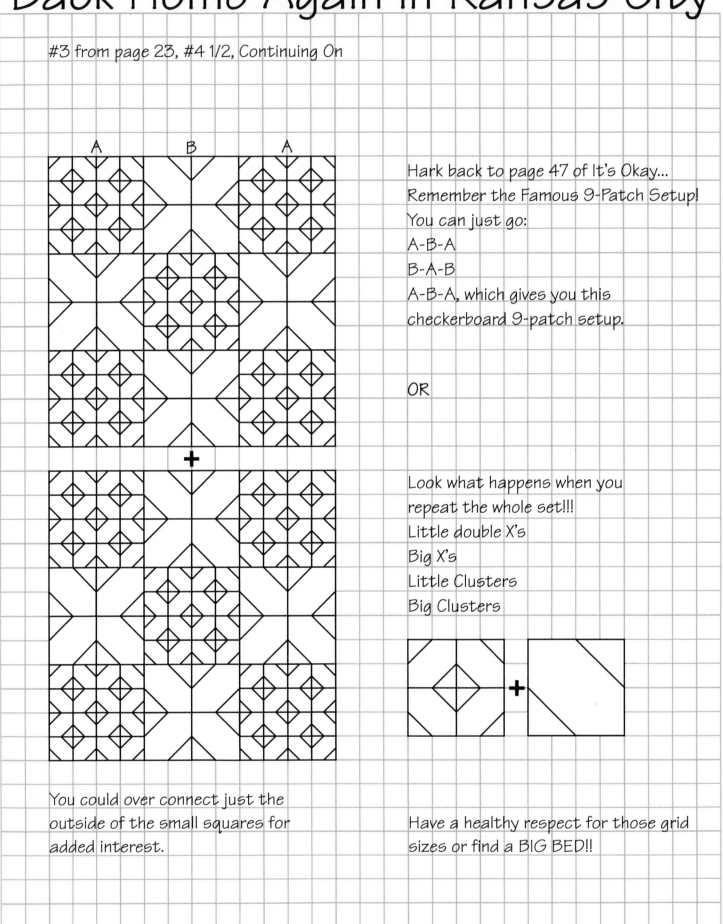

Hark back to page 47 of It's Okay...
Remember the Famous 9-Patch Setup!
You can just go:
A-B-A
B-A-B
A-B-A, which gives you this
checkerboard 9-patch setup.

OR

Look what happens when you
repeat the whole set!!!
Little double X's
Big X's
Little Clusters
Big Clusters

You could over connect just the
outside of the small squares for
added interest.

Have a healthy respect for those grid
sizes or find a BIG BED!!

Back Home Again, Continued

Make 320 Small Connector Blocks

Make 64 Large Connector Blocks

Dugout Workout

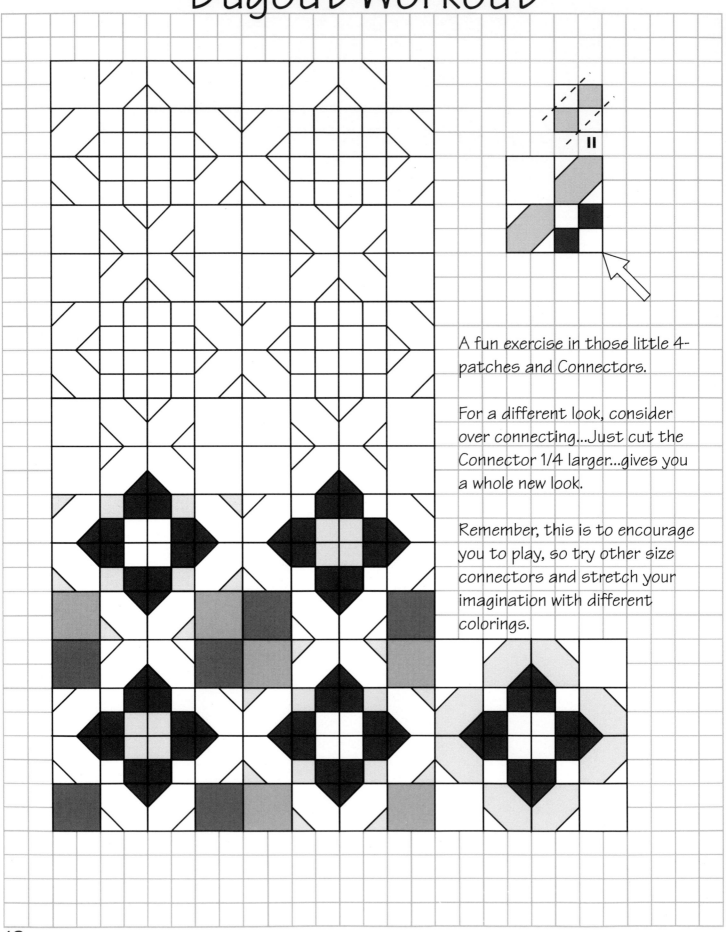

A fun exercise in those little 4-patches and Connectors.

For a different look, consider over connecting...Just cut the Connector 1/4 larger...gives you a whole new look.

Remember, this is to encourage you to play, so try other size connectors and stretch your imagination with different colorings.

MISSI**S**IPPI

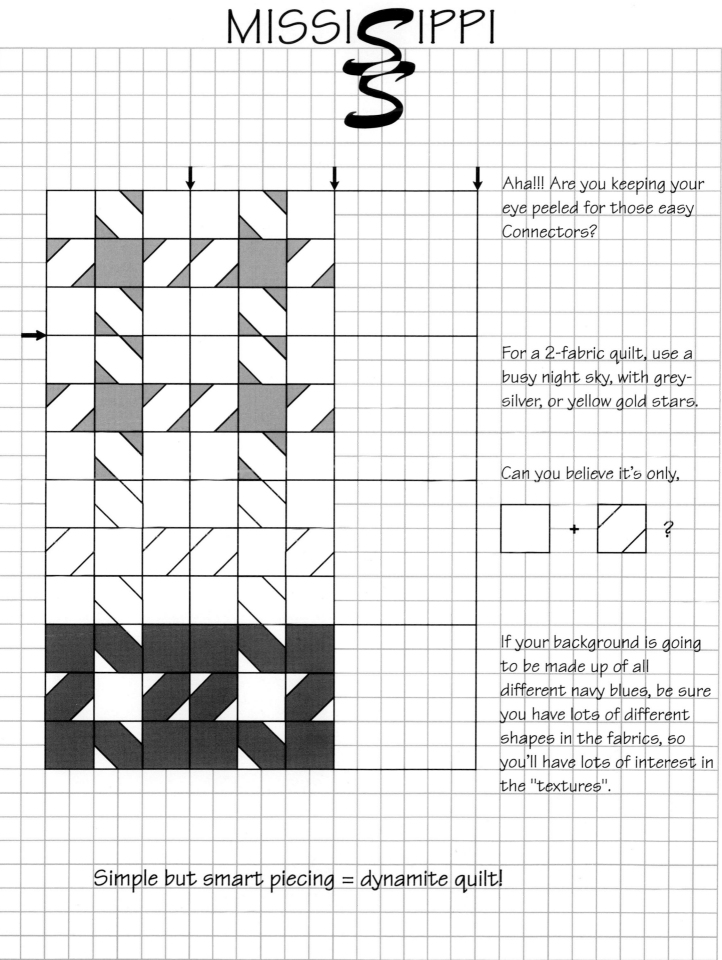

Aha!!! Are you keeping your eye peeled for those easy Connectors?

For a 2-fabric quilt, use a busy night sky, with grey-silver, or yellow gold stars.

Can you believe it's only,

☐ + ◩ ?

If your background is going to be made up of all different navy blues, be sure you have lots of different shapes in the fabrics, so you'll have lots of interest in the "textures".

Simple but smart piecing = dynamite quilt!

Linked Star Medallion

Recognize this??? Yes, indeed, the old Linked Star again, (Page 48, It's Okay) only with different shading!

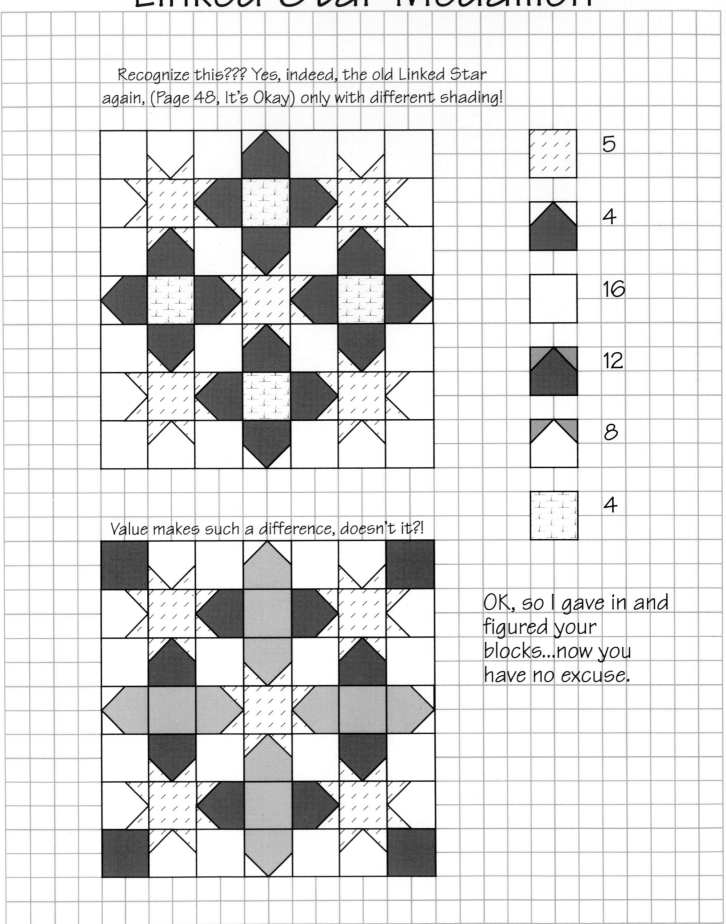

Value makes such a difference, doesn't it?!

	5
	4
	16
	12
	8
	4

OK, so I gave in and figured your blocks...now you have no excuse.

"Do You Want Instant?" #2*

Stars made with connectors, simple
connector blocks and unpieced blocks.

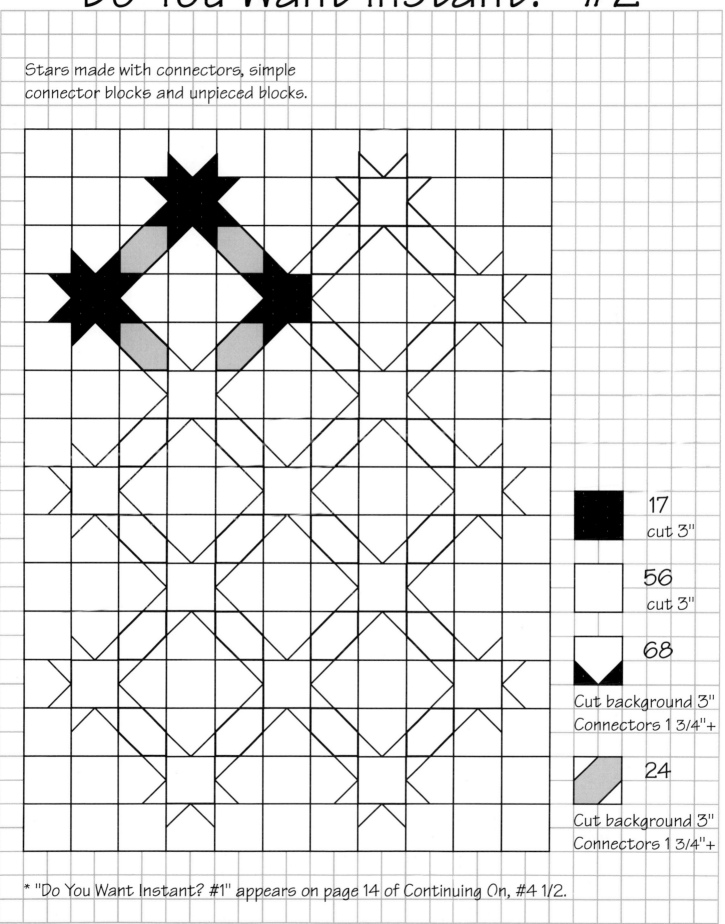

■	17 cut 3"
□	56 cut 3"
▽	68 Cut background 3" Connectors 1 3/4"+
◹	24 Cut background 3" Connectors 1 3/4"+

* "Do You Want Instant? #1" appears on page 14 of Continuing On, #4 1/2.

"Do You Want Instant?" #2
For Upper-Classmen

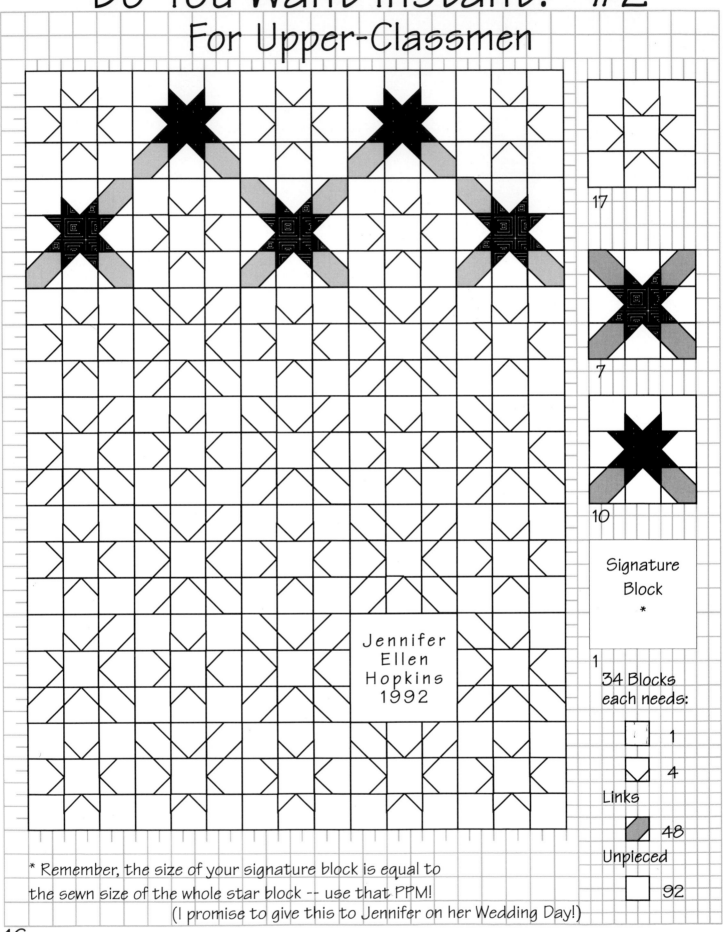

17

7

10

Signature
Block
*

1

34 Blocks
each needs:

☐ 1

◹ 4

Links

◪ 48

Unpieced

☐ 92

Jennifer
Ellen
Hopkins
1992

* Remember, the size of your signature block is equal to

the sewn size of the whole star block -- use that PPM!

(I promise to give this to Jennifer on her Wedding Day!)

"Do You Want Instant?" #2
for Over-Achievers

(This really isn't instant...but it IS easy!)

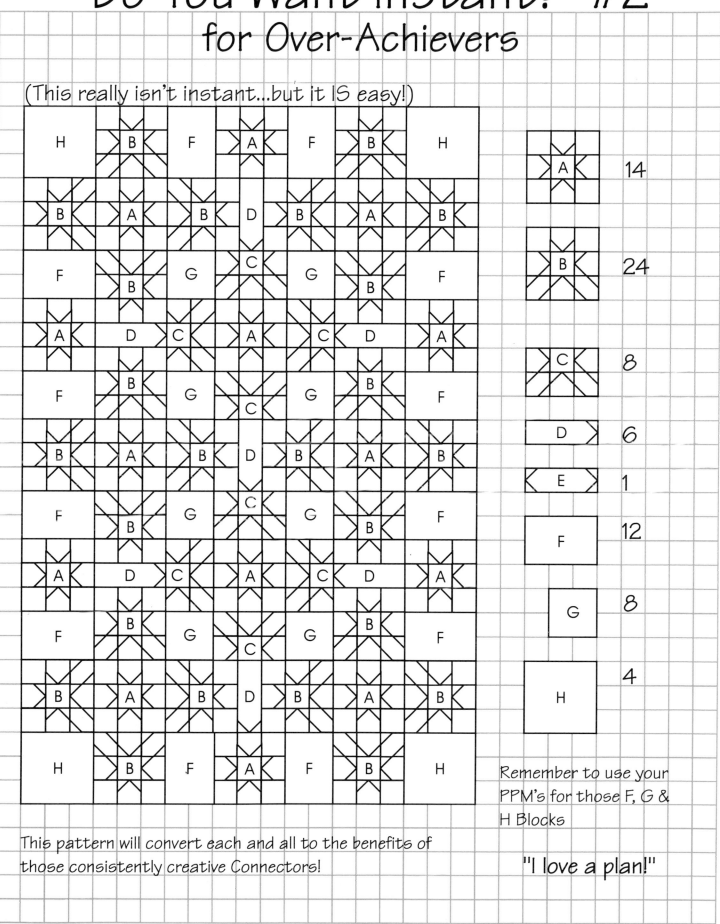

Block	Count
A	14
B	24
C	8
D	6
E	1
F	12
G	8
H	4

Remember to use your PPM's for those F, G & H Blocks

This pattern will convert each and all to the benefits of those consistently creative Connectors!

"I love a plan!"

"A Simple, But Snazzy Incorporated Border"

The trick of this pattern....
use your favorite block from the
It's Okay If You Sit On My Quilt Book
such as Card Trick used here.

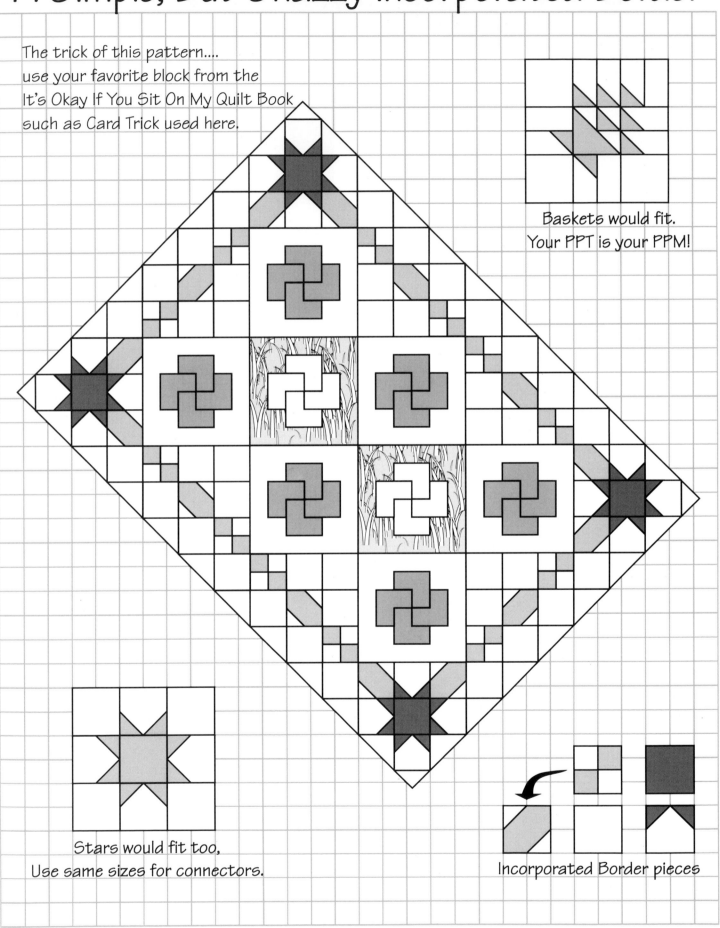

Baskets would fit.
Your PPT is your PPM!

Stars would fit too,
Use same sizes for connectors.

Incorporated Border pieces

"Heart with Star Center Rosette"

All PPM's and those marvelous Connectors!

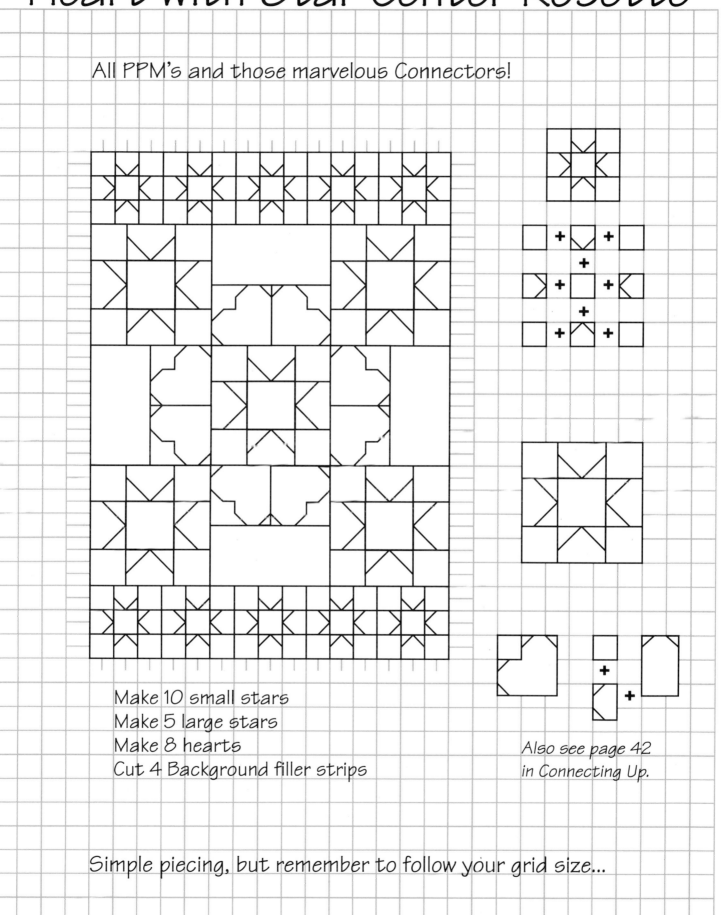

Make 10 small stars
Make 5 large stars
Make 8 hearts
Cut 4 Background filler strips

Also see page 42
in Connecting Up.

Simple piecing, but remember to follow your grid size...

Let's Take a Break

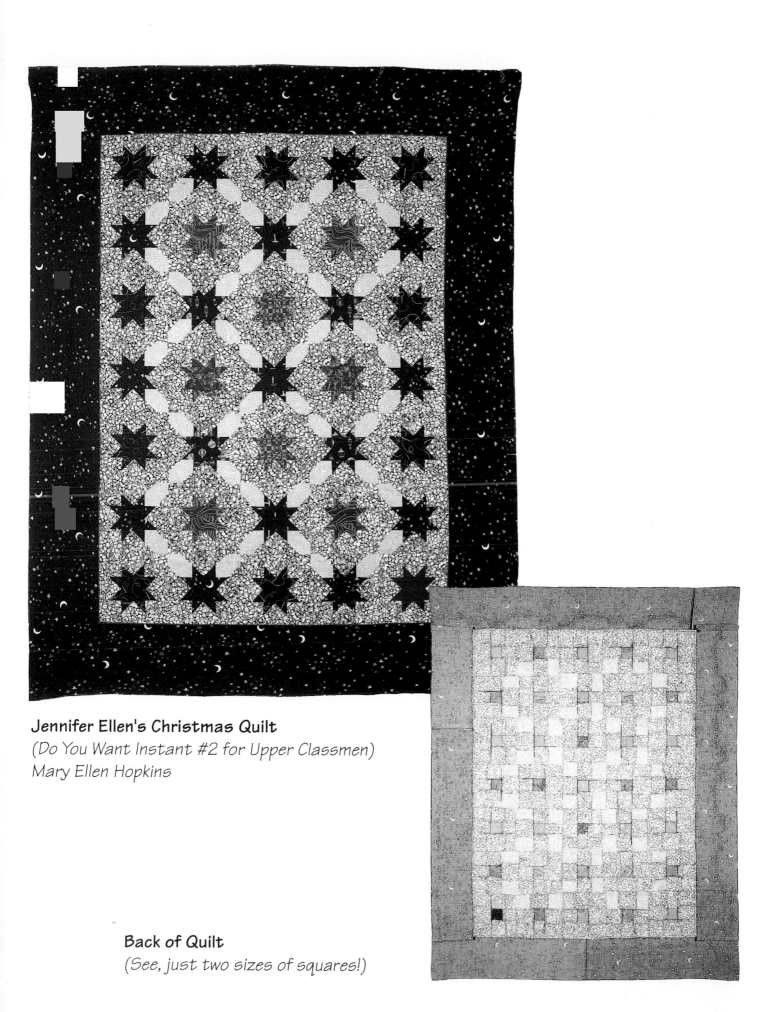

Jennifer Ellen's Christmas Quilt
(Do You Want Instant #2 for Upper Classmen)
Mary Ellen Hopkins

Back of Quilt
(See, just two sizes of squares!)

Hearts & Star Center Rosette

Joanna Myrick
Quilts & Other Pleasures
Atascadero, California

Hearts & Star Center Rosette

Dawn Sarrault
Ice House
Grayling, Michigan

Cherries, Cherries, Cherries (40's Style)

Terri Gunn, Kathleen Springer, Gachia Hoefer,
Kaye England
Quilt Quarters
Carmel, Indiana

Kansas City Dugout
Pat Farace
Warren, New Jersey

Kansas City Dugout
Kaye England
Quilt Quarters
Carmel, Indiana

Snowball Ph.D.. (Variation 1)
Caroline Berk
Quilts & Other Pleasures
Atascadero, California

Snowball Ph.D. (Variation 2)
Jean Humanesky
Country Peddler
St. Paul, Minnesota

Cross My Heart
Margaret Prina
Quiltworks
Albuquerque, New Mexico

Shaded Gardens
Carolyn Reese
Fabric Patch
Montclair, California

A Simple, But Snazzy Incorporated Border
Jan Krueger
Hearthside Quilters Nook
Hales Corners, Wisconsin

Back Home Again in Kansas City
Jan Krueger
Hearthside Quilters Nook
Hales Corners, Wisconsin

Linked Star Medallion
Lydia Quigley
Kingston, Ontario

Laughing All The Way
Mary Ellen Hopkins

Laughing All The Way
Fabrics by Mary Ellen Hopkins

Santa Monica Star
Mary Ellen Hopkins

Santa Monica Medallion/
Kansas City Dugout Border
Kaye England
Quilt Quarters
Carmel, Indiana

Santa Monica Star
Karin Sheard
Crazy Ladies
Santa Monica, California

OK, Back to Play!

Santa Monica Star

This block reminds me of our spectacular Santa Monica skies!

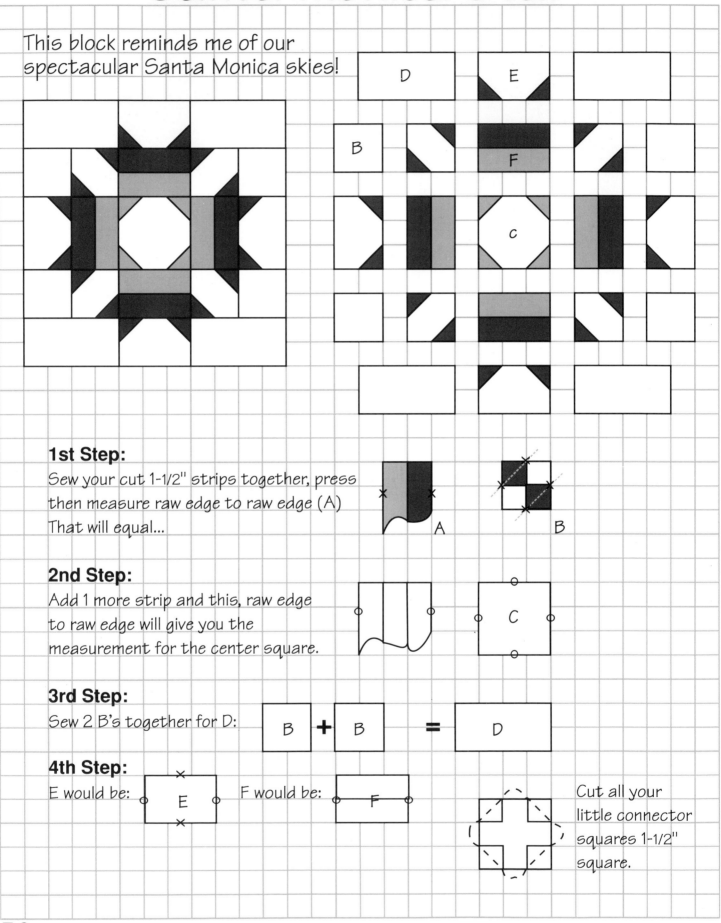

1st Step:

Sew your cut 1-1/2" strips together, press then measure raw edge to raw edge (A) That will equal...

2nd Step:

Add 1 more strip and this, raw edge to raw edge will give you the measurement for the center square.

3rd Step:

Sew 2 B's together for D: B + B = D

4th Step:

E would be: F would be:

Cut all your little connector squares 1-1/2" square.

Some More Santa Monica Stars

Santa Monica Medallion

This star offers lots of design choices for medallions or borders. Plan your own unique stars (you could even name them after your favorite city)!

"Friendship Spools"

What could be more appropriate for quilters, but bunches of colorful spools, of course using striped fabrics for the "thread".

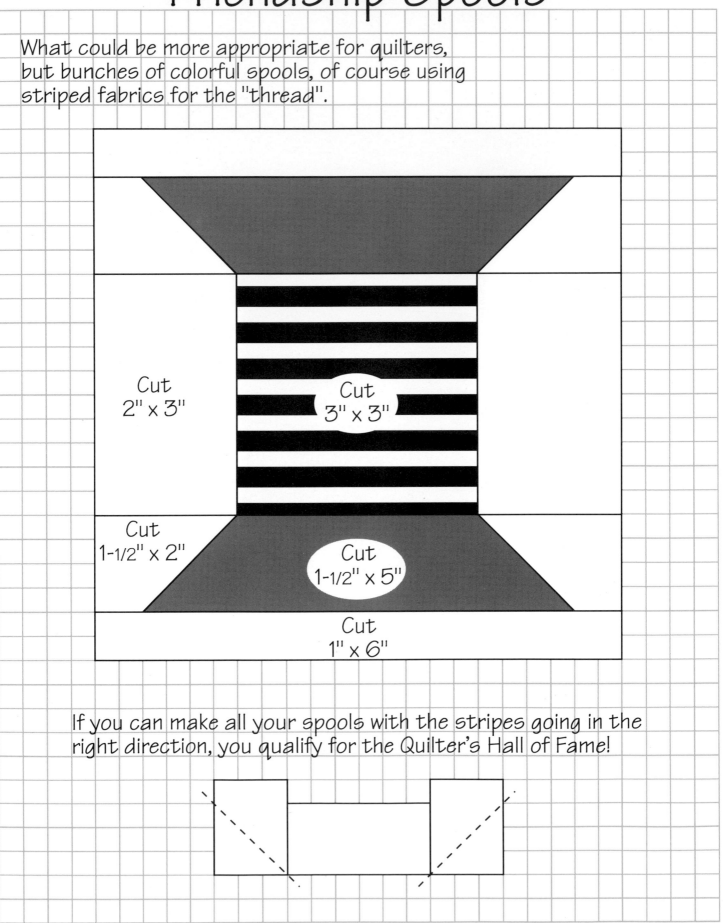

Cut
2" x 3"

Cut
3" x 3"

Cut
1-1/2" x 2"

Cut
1-1/2" x 5"

Cut
1" x 6"

If you can make all your spools with the stripes going in the right direction, you qualify for the Quilter's Hall of Fame!

Spools From Your Friends

Sharing Striped Fabric

Each 4-Spool Block could have its own background fabric.
The floater can be trimmed to designated size.

Every block would have to be square to do this set and filler strips would be needed on some rows

You could always make the stripes by top-stitching or quilting them in!

Cherries, Cherries, Cherries

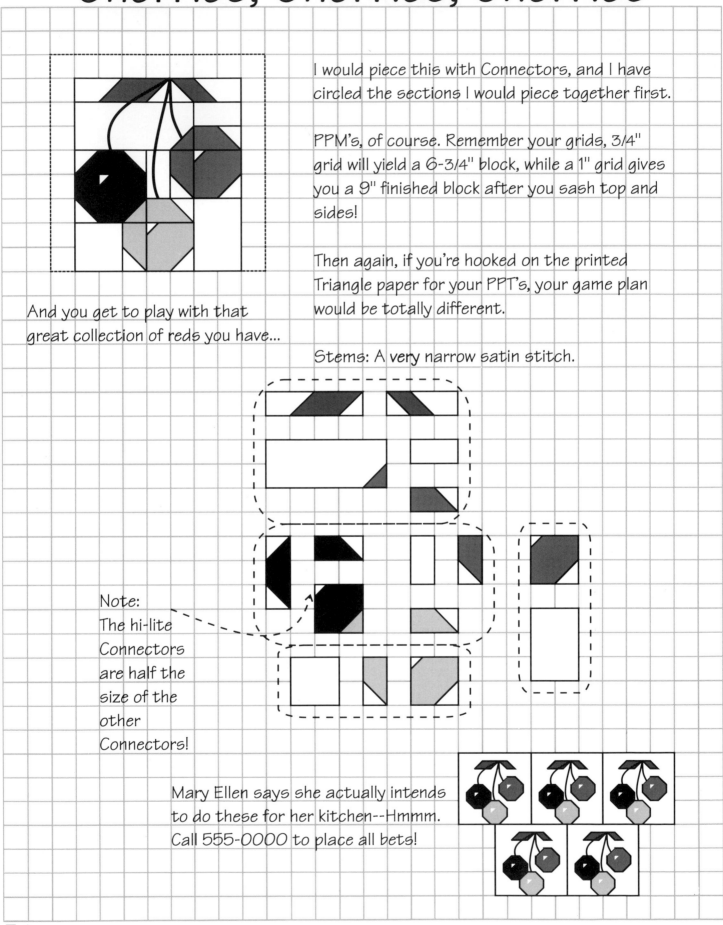

I would piece this with Connectors, and I have circled the sections I would piece together first.

PPM's, of course. Remember your grids, 3/4" grid will yield a 6-3/4" block, while a 1" grid gives you a 9" finished block after you sash top and sides!

Then again, if you're hooked on the printed Triangle paper for your PPT's, your game plan would be totally different.

Stems: A very narrow satin stitch.

And you get to play with that great collection of reds you have...

Note:
The hi-lite Connectors are half the size of the other Connectors!

Mary Ellen says she actually intends to do these for her kitchen--Hmmm. Call 555-0000 to place all bets!

"Snowball PH.D."

Before you pass over this quilt, check out the photo.

(Kindergarten Piecing)

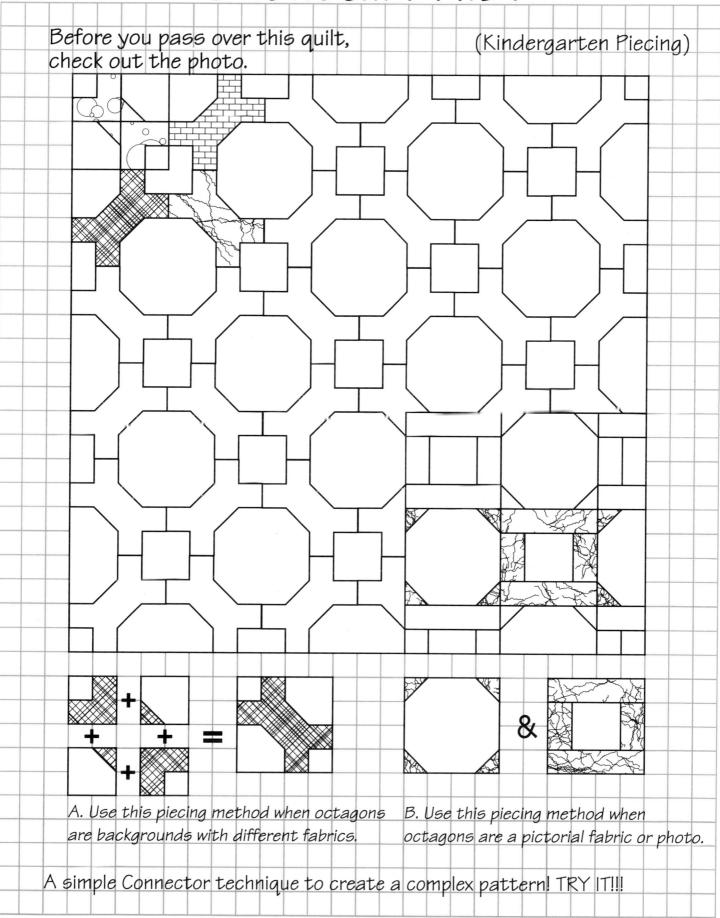

A. Use this piecing method when octagons are backgrounds with different fabrics.

B. Use this piecing method when octagons are a pictorial fabric or photo.

A simple Connector technique to create a complex pattern! TRY IT!!!

"An Exercise On Those PPM's"
Chained Hearts

Step 1: Determine what this will equal...

Step 2: Make this first, press, measure raw edge to raw edge for...

Step 3:

Step 4: Piece these sections together for Block A

Step 5: Piece the heart section of Block B, (minus the 2 side strips).*

Step 6: On your first Heart section, sew on side strips that you know will be too wide. Press and then trim down to fit Block A.

Step 7: Turn Block B to wrong side, measure the side strips, cut remaining side strips this size.

A

B

Border Block
(See Drawing)

Chained Hearts

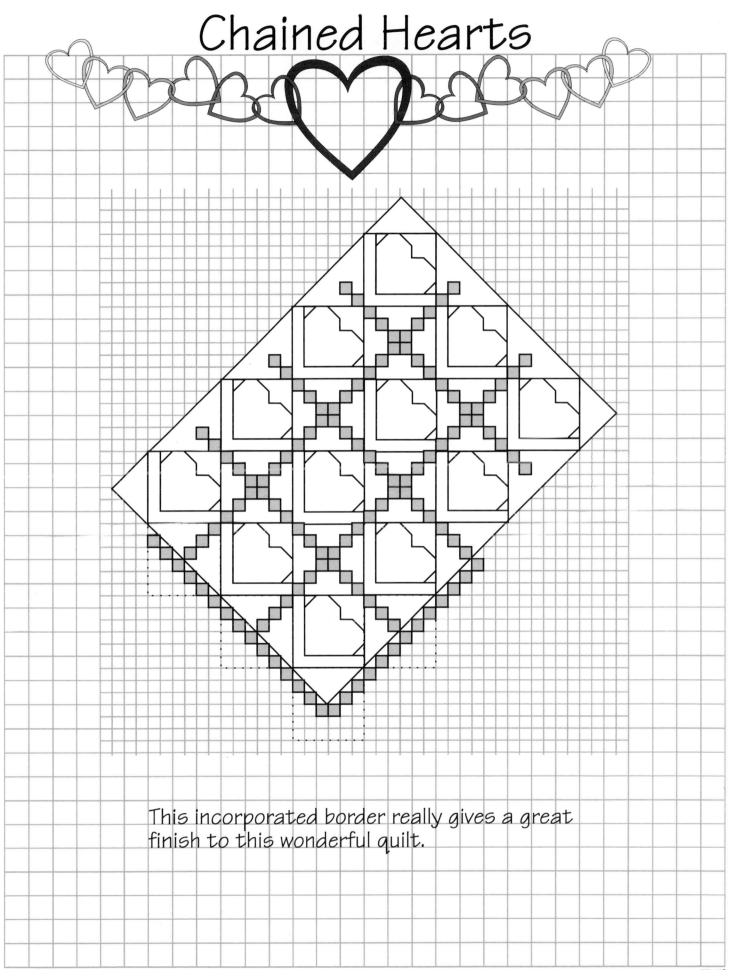

This incorporated border really gives a great
finish to this wonderful quilt.

"Cross My Heart"

Yes, Indeed, Page 25 of It's Okay, again...

Simple piecing, but your shading and choice of fabrics will show off your expertise.

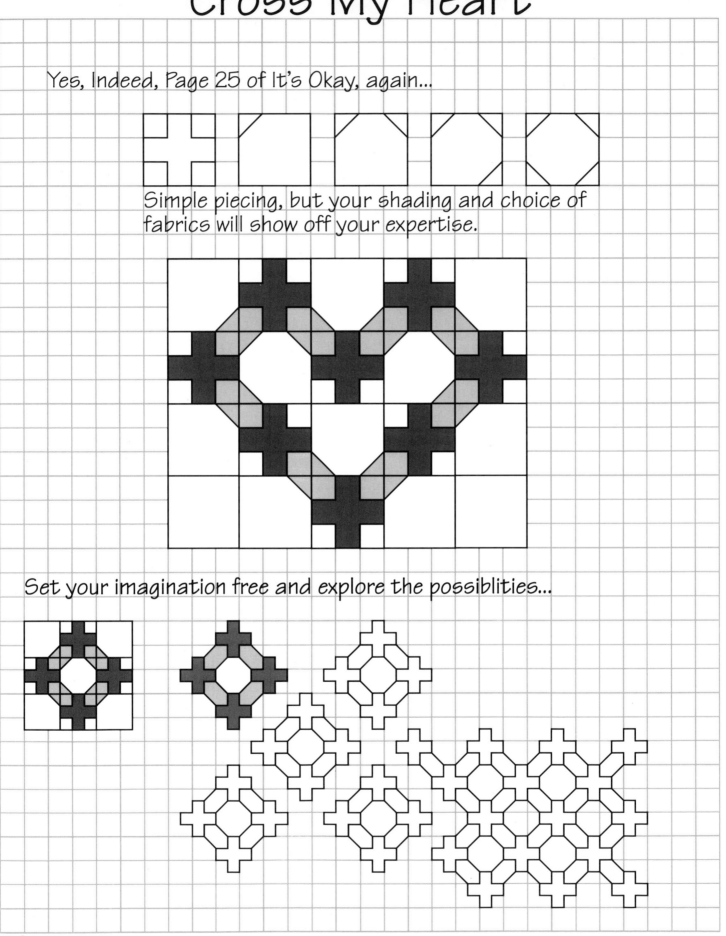

Set your imagination free and explore the possiblities...

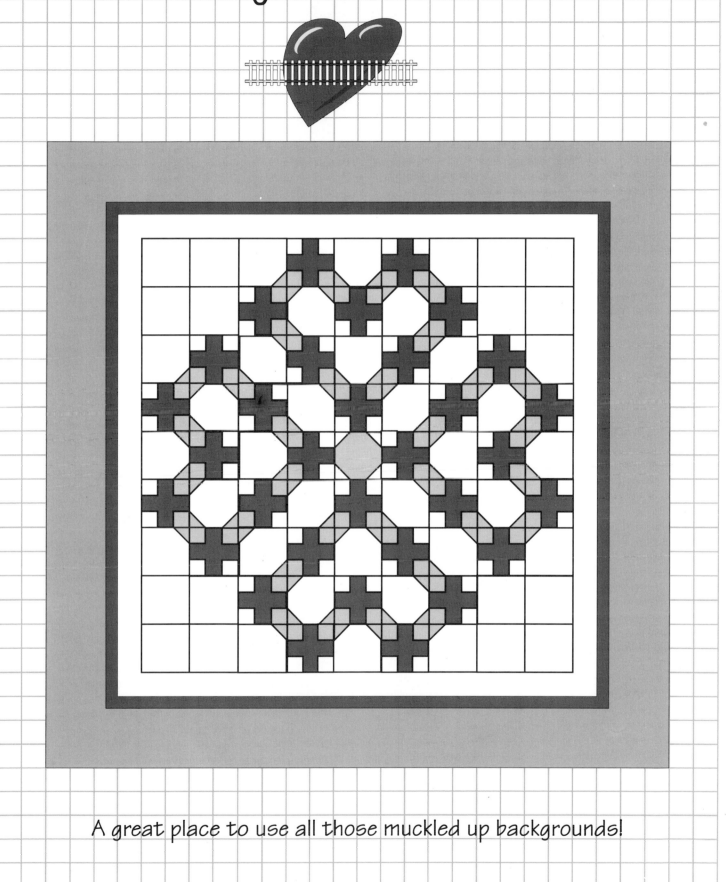

A great place to use all those muckled up backgrounds!

"Shaded Gardens"

Remember the Checklist on
Page 2 in the It's Okay book!

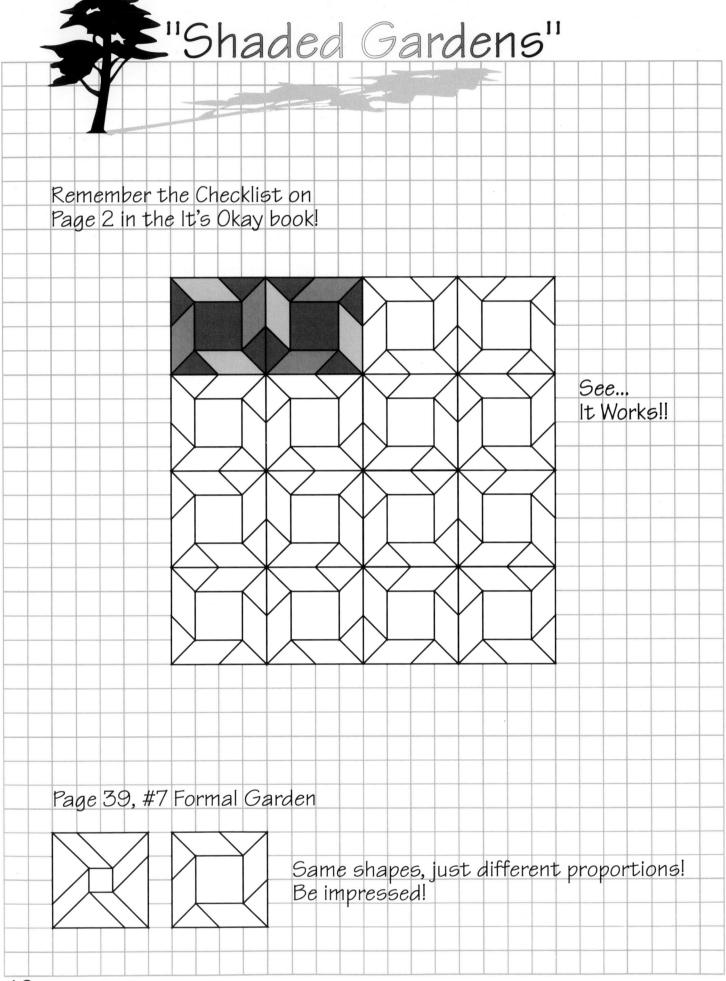

See...
It Works!!

Page 39, #7 Formal Garden

Same shapes, just different proportions!
Be impressed!

Shady Instructions

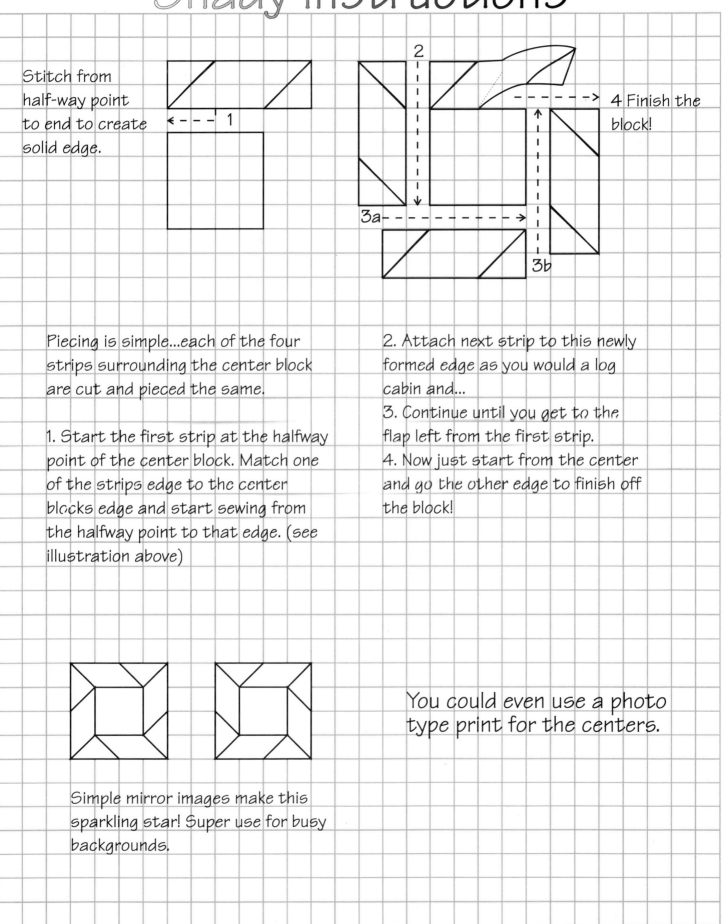

Stitch from half-way point to end to create solid edge.

1

2

3a

3b

4 Finish the block!

Piecing is simple...each of the four strips surrounding the center block are cut and pieced the same.

1. Start the first strip at the halfway point of the center block. Match one of the strips edge to the center blocks edge and start sewing from the halfway point to that edge. (see illustration above)

2. Attach next strip to this newly formed edge as you would a log cabin and...
3. Continue until you get to the flap left from the first strip.
4. Now just start from the center and go the other edge to finish off the block!

Simple mirror images make this sparkling star! Super use for busy backgrounds.

You could even use a photo type print for the centers.

"Laughing All The Way"
thru Switzerland, Australia & the Caribbean!

This has become one of my favorite piecing projects!

O, X, ☆ = background fabric
(can be different fabrics or all the same)

"Oh, I just love that "It's Okay" book and those fabulous connectors!"

| 4 | 8 | 4 | 8 | 1 |

Make your PPM first (4-patch)
Can be done with scraps or just five fabrics.

Dear Mary Ellen,

Dear Mary Ellen,
How do you

Thank you,

Dear Mary Ellen,

You all know by now that I do concept books and therefore don't usually include how-to directions for basic quiltmaking skills, however, after receiving many requests for my favorite tips, I have decided to include some I feel most necessary for a great finished project.

Question:
Mary Ellen, how do you keep your quilt corners so square?

Answer:
Most sewers do a good job on their basic quilt and then begin adding borders and shortly realize they have made a wave instead. Listen UP for a solution.

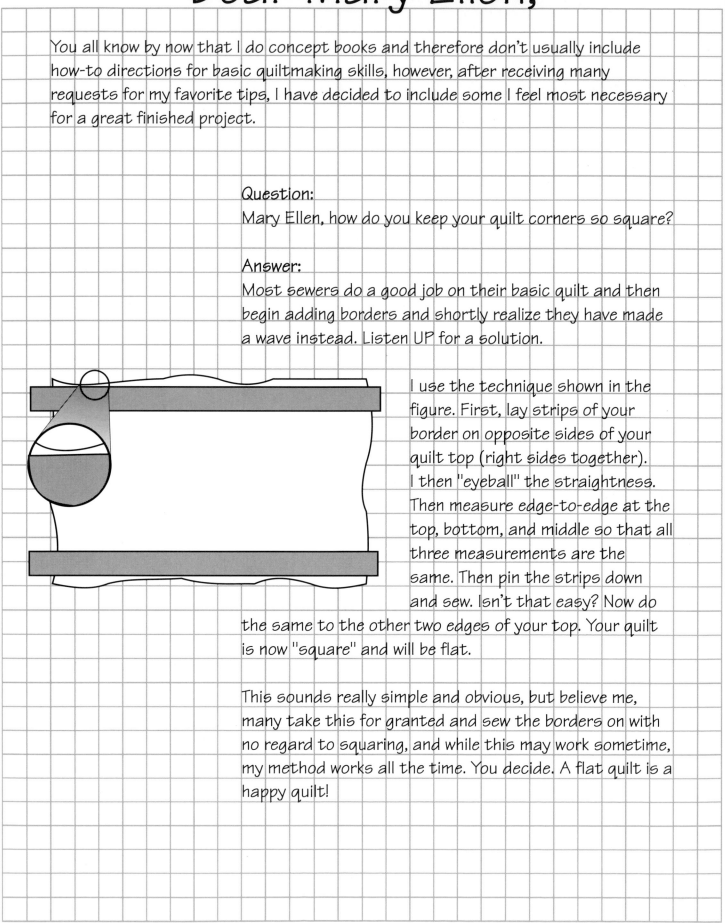

I use the technique shown in the figure. First, lay strips of your border on opposite sides of your quilt top (right sides together). I then "eyeball" the straightness. Then measure edge-to-edge at the top, bottom, and middle so that all three measurements are the same. Then pin the strips down and sew. Isn't that easy? Now do the same to the other two edges of your top. Your quilt is now "square" and will be flat.

This sounds really simple and obvious, but believe me, many take this for granted and sew the borders on with no regard to squaring, and while this may work sometime, my method works all the time. You decide. A flat quilt is a happy quilt!

Dear Mary Ellen,

Question:

OK, Mary Ellen, I see how you keep your borders straight, but how do you get the quilt so flat to begin with.

Answer:

Many of you have already yelled out the answer, but just in case someone in the Arctic hasn't heard of this, the famous two-sie, four-sie setup. Read on...

I never sew anything together until I have my entire piece on a board, or the floor (try those foam core boards, yeah, I said it) and then I proceed by sewing all the squares together in twos, then join into fours, then eights, then sixteens, and so forth forming bigger sections. This allows you to eliminate all those seams running across or down the quilt (and you can usually see these, especially in a diagonal setting) and only have one cross or vertical seam the length or width of the quilt. I have found this to be the most effective way of piecing all the blocks together. The secret is in picking up the rows orderly and following the same sequence.

You will of course have an odd block sometimes, so just incorporate it into the last row you piece, so you will have to join this last row as a three-sie, see, no problem!

Important! Make all of your twosie's first, then your foursies, etc.

The following two pages are graph paper for you to use while planning your next masterpiece quilting project. Enjoy!!

Twosie's

Foursie's

Eightsie's, & so on and so on

Personal Private Showcase Grids

Personal Private Showcase Grids

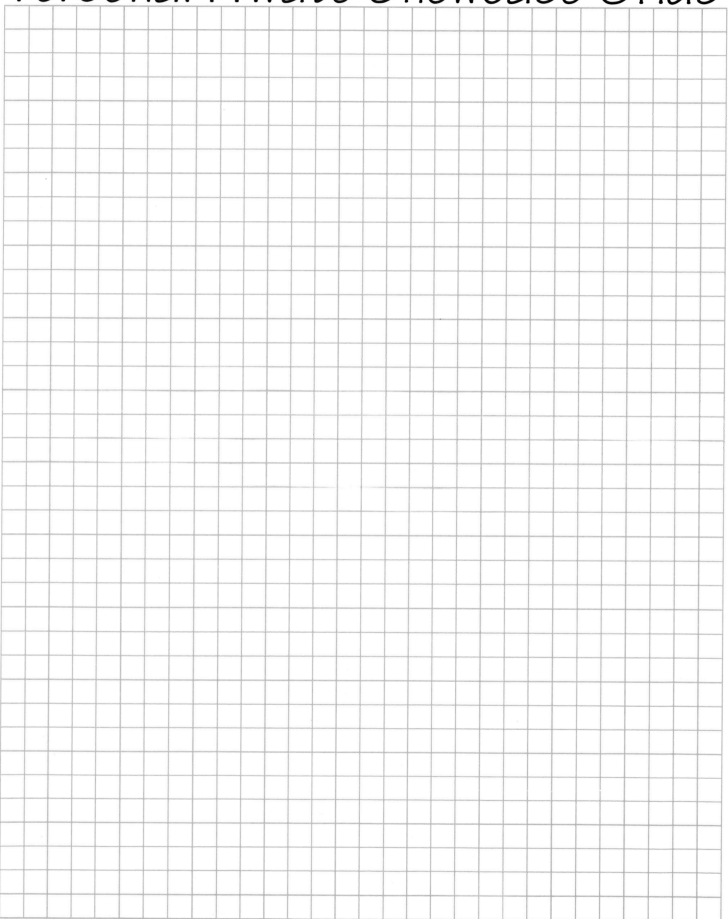

About the Author...

Mary Ellen Hopkins is a quilter, author, fabric designer, shop owner, publisher, lecturer and teacher residing in Santa Monica, California. Mary Ellen has a reputation for the incredibly enthusiastic way she spreads the message about her trademark "Personal Private" way of designing and making quilts. Inspired by her spectacular view of the Pacific Ocean, she continues to produce top notch quilt designs, fabric designs and much inspiration for the quilting world.

Mary Ellen's Crazy Ladies and Friends quilt shop in Santa Monica, California offers a Fabric-of-the-Month Club, retail mail-order service and is the homebase for her speaking engagements and hands-on teaching seminars she conducts around the world for consumers and shop owners. Please contact Crazy Ladies and Friends, 1604 Santa Monica Boulevard, Santa Monica, California 90404, (310-828-3122) for more information.